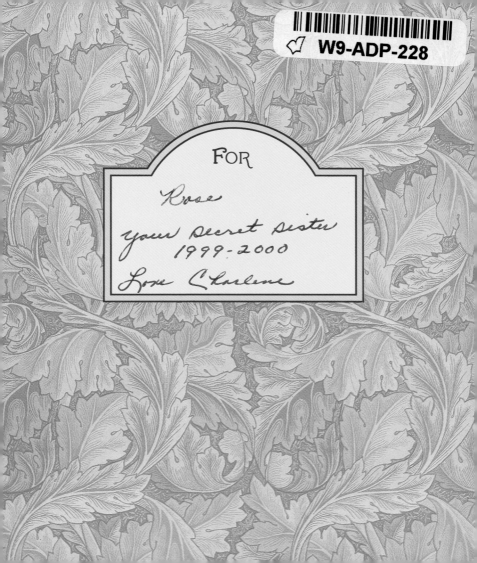

FOR

Rose

Your secret sister
1999-2000

Love Charlene

Loving Kindness
Lend a Helping Hand

by Sophia Bedford-Pierce

Photographs by Jill Sabella and Solomon M. Skolnick,
hand-painted by Jill Sabella
Book design and illustration by Mullen & Katz

PETER PAUPER PRESS, INC.
WHITE PLAINS, NEW YORK

The publisher wishes to thank our stars:
Chloe, Izaac, Kate, Oliver, Sarah, Sophia, and Wiley

Cover photo by Solomon M. Skolnick,
hand painted by Jill Sabella
Cover designed by Mullen & Katz

Loving Kindness:

Lend a Helping Hand

Introduction

Grandma Sophie's legacy took many forms. Amongst the treasures that she bestowed on me were a hammer (and of course a bag of nails), a tape measure, a needle, a thimble, instructions on how to craft a dozen types of knots, gardening gloves, a love of hats, and her diaries. Of all the treasures that she gave to me, however, the most precious was her ability to teach by example.

Grandma really believed that every person was special, and that doing for others, often even before doing for oneself, was important. She explained that every time you extended yourself for a friend, a neighbor, or even a stranger, you brought something of value into their lives.

I often re-read Sophie's diaries. And as I do, the voice of a happy and wise woman who loved the fullness of life speaks to me again and again. "Every gracious act enriches the world," she would say. What Grandma Sophie gave to me I gladly share with you.

S. B-P.

Each in
her turn
has the means
to build a
better world.

We are
beings who are
made for
sharing.

What
you give of
yourself is
greater than
any other
gift.

Sharing requires
loving another
more than you
knew you could love.

What we
do for
each other
we do
gladly.

Tender acts of kindness
cannot be commanded;
they are given freely
or not at all.

Charity
is blind to
color, blind to
age, and to
all other
forms
of outward
appearance.

Do what you do
with care,
and its value
will be
apparent.

Sharing your good fortune makes the world a little brighter.

A caring person
walks on the path
to wisdom.

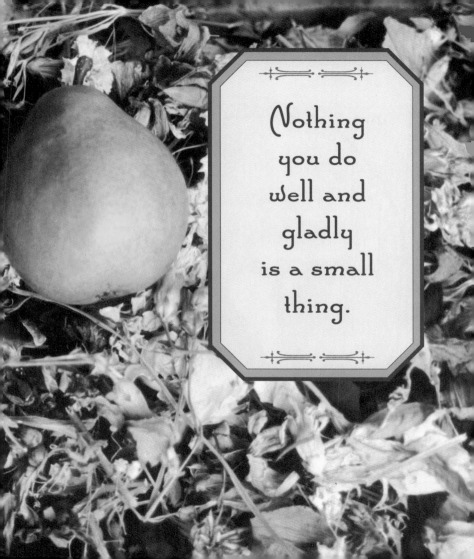

Nothing
you do
well and
gladly
is a small
thing.

Busy your hands,
Open your heart,
Share what
you have created.

You can help someone
far more effectively
if you try to give her
what she is asking for,
rather than
giving only what
you think
you have to give.

Many nails are needed
to build a house,
just as it takes
more than one good deed
to create goodness.

When you
teach well
you also
learn,
and all
are richer
for it.

Compassion
does not come
in a box with
a pretty bow;
it is the act of
an enlightened mind,
and a full heart.

When you think less
about yourself,
you often
think more
of yourself.

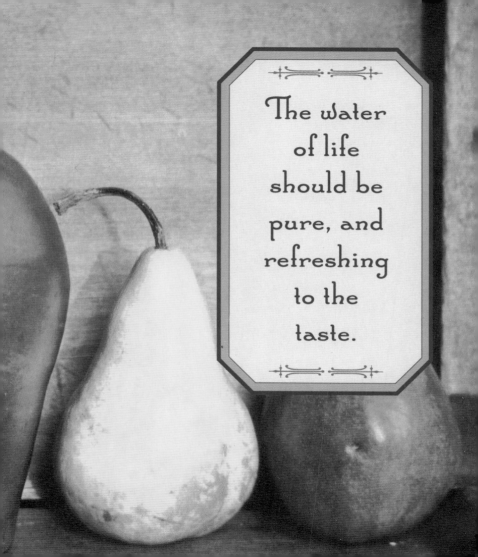

The water
of life
should be
pure, and
refreshing
to the
taste.

Feed a person
who is hungry, but also
teach him how to
plant a seed.
The gift of self-reliance
will give him the means
to prosper and to
help others in turn.

A person's
true wealth
is measured
in blessings.

Be
gracious to
those who
visit your
home and
you will
always have
shelter.

How you walk along your path,
and what you leave for others
to find, is the measure of
your journey.